FĪRE's GUIDE TO
STUDENT FEES, FUNDING, AND
LEGAL EQUALITY ON CAMPUS

FIRE's GUIDES TO
STUDENT RIGHTS ON CAMPUS

www.thefireguides.org

FIRE's Guide to Religious Liberty on Campus

FIRE's Guide to Student Fees, Funding, and Legal Equality on Campus

FIRE's Guide to Due Process and Fair Procedure on Campus

FIRE's Guide to Free Speech on Campus

FIRE's Guide to First-Year Orientation and to Thought Reform on Campus

FIRE's Guide to the Rights of Faculty

FIRE

FIRE's GUIDE TO

STUDENT FEES, FUNDING, AND LEGAL EQUALITY ON CAMPUS

Jordan Lorence

FOUNDATION FOR INDIVIDUAL RIGHTS IN EDUCATION
Philadelphia

FIRE's Know Your Rights Program and FIRE's *Guides* to Student Rights on Campus are made possible by grants from The Achelis Foundation, The Joseph Harrison Jackson Foundation, and Earhart Foundation. The Foundation for Individual Rights in Education gratefully acknowledges their support.

ISBN 0-9724712-1-9

Lorence, Jordan.
  FIRE's guide to student fees, funding, and legal equality on campus / Jordan Lorence.
     p. cm.
  ISBN 0-9724712-1-9 (alk. paper)
  1. College students--Civil rights--United States. 2. Liberty of conscience--United States. 3. College costs--Law and legislation--United States.
I. Foundation for Individual Rights in Education. II. Title: Guide to student fees, funding, and legal equality on campus. III. Title.
KF4243.L67 2002
344.73'0793--dc21

Published in the United States of America by:

> Foundation for Individual Rights in Education
> 210 West Washington Square, Suite 303
> Philadelphia, PA 19106

Cover Illustration by Glenn Pierce

Cover and Interior design by Eliz. Anne O'Donnell

Printed in the United States of America

CONTENTS

PREFACE

Students should know their rights and liberties, and they need to be better informed and better equipped about how to assert and defend these precious things. The protectors of students' rights and liberties—those faculty, administrators, parents, alumni, friends, citizens, advisers, and attorneys who care about such vital matters— should understand the threats to freedom and legal equality on our campuses, the moral and legal means of combating those threats, and the acquired experience of recent years. To that end, the Foundation for Individual Rights in Education (FIRE) offers this *Guide to Student Fees, Funding, and Legal Equality on Campus*, part of a series of such guides designed to restore individual rights and the values of a free society to our nation's colleges and universities. These guides also should remind those who write, revise, and enforce campus policies of the legal and moral constraints that restrict their authority. The sooner that colleges and universities understand their legal and moral obligations to a free and decent society, the less need there will be for guides such as these.

INTRODUCTION

Many students attending public colleges and universities are surprised and sometimes outraged to learn that school rules require them to fund groups that advocate ideas they find morally or politically unacceptable, across the spectrum of student organizations. Mandatory fees, the funding of student groups, and the often arbitrary standards by which such funding occurs raise issues of the highest constitutional and moral importance. Students, faculty, and administrators should understand the principles involved in these issues. Students who believe themselves the victims of unlawful behaviors and double standards should understand their rights, the limits of those rights, and the means to seek a more just campus.

Students on many campuses understand that the fees they must pay are often used to fund groups that advocate a wide array of beliefs and causes. Most campuses have some combination of groups composed of evangelical Christians; gay, lesbian, bisexual, and transgendered students; environmentalists; Latin mass Catholics; vegetarians; Muslims; atheists; feminists; anarchists; communists; or conservatives (in addition, indeed, to bagpipers and chess players). Many students ask, "How can the school force me, as a condition of my getting an education here, to fund groups with which I don't agree?" Starting in the 1970s, students at public colleges and universities have brought numerous lawsuits that asserted, on First Amendment grounds, the right of individual students to opt out of having to fund groups that they find objectionable. The results of such suits are finally becoming clear.

More recently, student fee controversies have generated another category of lawsuit. These suits have focused on the issue of whether or not a state university—or its student government—may *deny* funding to a campus organization because it advocates a controversial point of view, such as salvation in Jesus Christ alone, absolute tolerance toward homosexuals, or either side of the affirmative action debate. Again, the courts are now speaking with a clearer voice.

A BRIEF HISTORY OF
MANDATORY STUDENT FEES

Student fees arose on America's campuses over a century ago. Students on many campuses decided collectively to assess a fee on themselves in order to fund extracurricular activities and niceties that were not covered by tuition. The belief was that certain activities and facilities—from athletic fields to student centers to caps and gowns—clearly would enhance student life on campus. For example, in 1875, the student fee at the University of Wisconsin paid for "heating and lighting the university hall and public rooms, music, each diploma, and a matriculation fee in the law department." Similarly, in 1949, the fee paid for "admission to athletic contests, concerts, class dues, cap and gown fees, [and] science laboratory fees."

Mandatory student fees first became controversial during the 1960s and early 1970s. During those turbulent Vietnam War years, student activists began to see these fees as a potential source of funding for their various political and ideological causes. Some activists ran for office in student government and, once elected, they dramatically changed how student fees were given out to campus groups. Where student fees traditionally had been used only to pay for noncontroversial services that most or all students could use, they now became a means of backing the ideological advocacy of what critics saw as special interest groups. To those favoring such new uses of student fees, the argument remained that they added to the quality of student life. To opponents of such uses, the argument was that one group of students was forcing another group of students to pay for causes in which they might not believe, or, indeed, to which they strongly objected.

In the late 1960s and early 1970s, Ralph Nader helped to bring about this change when he and his supporters started Public Interest Research Groups (PIRGs, as they have come to be known), based in individual states. PIRGs generally advocated controversial views on various environmental and consumer issues, and their activities included (and still include) aggressive lobbying of state legislatures and Congress to support their agendas. Nader's PIRG activists successfully convinced many colleges and universities to use referenda as a means to decide the PIRG's claims upon student fees, arguing that a majority of students could vote to impose an assessment that each student was then required to pay. This led many students to object. Some objected to being required to pay for political or moral activity they opposed. Others objected to the way groups were funded—by the choices of those few who controlled the student government or the disbursement of student fees. Defenders of the new funding justified it on the traditional grounds of enhancing student life.

Because mandatory student fees funded PIRGs and their controversial activism, such fees often became the focus of campus controversy about whether or not students could be compelled to fund politically partisan or activist groups. As early as 1974, the Wisconsin Attorney General questioned the constitutionality of the University of Wisconsin's recent decision to require students to pay a mandatory fee supporting a PIRG, but this did not lead to any ban on such a requirement.

At most campuses, during the Vietnam War era, the decision to fund the local PIRG soon spread to include the funding by mandatory fees of other ideological and political groups on campus, especially those that advocated liberal views on feminism, the environment, gay rights, and abortion. In these politically turbulent times, activists found mandatory student fees a welcome source of funds.

In the 1970s and 1980s, students who disapproved of mandatory contributions to activist campus organizations—especially to those with which they disagreed—

began filing lawsuits to opt out of funding PIRGs and other groups whose views and agendas they found objectionable. In a major case, *Galda v. Rutgers* (1985), students sued Rutgers (the State University of New Jersey) in federal court for the right not to pay a mandatory fee to NJPIRG, even though that fee was refundable to students who filled out forms expressing their ideological disagreement. The court dismissed Rutgers's argument that there were educational benefits associated with NJPIRG and found in favor of the students.

Similar suits have since been brought in New York and California. In *Carroll v. Blinken* (1992), students at The State University of New York at Albany sued in federal court for the right not to pay a mandatory fee to NYPIRG. The court found for the University, but it insisted in the ruling that the student fees paid to NYPIRG be spent on SUNY Albany students—something NYPIRG had not been doing. In *Smith v. Regents of the University of California* (1993), students at the University of California at Berkeley filed a lawsuit in state court opposing both the fee itself and how the fees were used by CALPIRG. The California Supreme Court upheld the University's right to assess a mandatory student fee, but it also found that using those fees to fund ideological groups violated the rights of students who opposed those groups' views. The ruling required the University of California Regents to offer refunds to students who did not want to pay for political and ideological activities.

Arguments became just as heated over issues of who received funding as they had become over the issue of who had to pay fees. Student officers and university administrators sometimes denied funding to groups they found "controversial." In 1988, the University of Arkansas did not fund a campus gay organization, on the grounds that it was "promoting" homosexuality. In *Gay and Lesbian Students Association v. Gohn*, however, the U.S. Court of Appeals for the Eighth Circuit required the University of Arkansas to fund the group, holding that the University had violated the First Amendment by denying funding to the group based on the specific viewpoint it espoused. In 1995, the United States Supreme Court, in *Rosenberger v. Rectors of the University of Virginia*, ruled that the University had violated the First Amendment by refusing to fund a campus evangelical newspaper because of its Christian views. The Supreme Court ruled that to deny a group funding because of the ideas that it advocates is an unconstitutional "viewpoint discrimination."

Mandatory student fees may have begun with the uncontroversial motive of funding extra amenities to enhance student life, such as student centers or athletic fields, but by the end of the twentieth century they had evolved into something extremely divisive, given their funding of ideological activism. Two recent Supreme Court decisions provide significant insight and direction both for students compelled to pay a mandatory fee and for campus organizations that seek funding from such student fee systems.

VIEWPOINT NEUTRALITY:
The Crucial Legal Concept in Assessing Mandatory Fees at Public Colleges and Universities

In two major cases, the U.S. Supreme Court has ruled that "viewpoint neutrality" governs both the distribution of student fees and the question of whether students may opt out of paying a mandatory fee. In the first case, *Rosenberger v. Rectors of the University of Virginia* (1995), the Court ruled that the University of Virginia violated the free speech rights of the student journalists producing a Christian campus newspaper when it denied that paper funding because of its "religious" views. In the second case, *Board of Regents of the University of Wisconsin System v. Southworth* (2000), the Court ruled that individual students have the right not to pay fees that fund groups they find objectionable if the university distributed money in a "viewpoint discriminatory" manner. In these cases taken together—*Rosenberger* and *Southworth*—the Court identified a vital constitutional principle that always must decide student fee disputes at public colleges and universities: a viewpoint neutrality that stands opposed to its opposite, "viewpoint discrimination."

Viewpoint neutrality is a well-known concept in First Amendment law. It stands for the idea that when government actions implicate the speech rights of groups and individuals, those actions must be done in an even-handed way. They may not discriminate **based on the message advocated**. Thus, a city has the power to prohibit all speakers from using bullhorns to amplify their speeches on public streets at three o'clock in the morning. If the city allows Republicans to make such speeches at that hour, however, it may not forbid Democrats from doing so too. Such viewpoint discrimination would be a deviation from the constitutional requirement of viewpoint neutrality. Viewpoint discrimination occurs when the government uses its power to advance one person's opinion over another's in such matters as religion, politics, and belief.

Rosenberger and *Southworth* establish the principle that a state university or college must distribute funds collected by mandatory student fees in a viewpoint neutral manner. State universities and colleges violate the right of free expression guaranteed by the First Amendment if they deny funding to a group because of the viewpoint it advocates, or if they require students to pay into a system whose official policies prohibit religious or political groups from receiving school funding. If a state university or college forbids its officials or agents from considering a group's viewpoint when deciding whether to fund it, then the school may require all students to pay fees. Together, the rulings show clearly that (1) any student organization at a state school that is denied funding because of its views can sue claiming viewpoint discrimination; and (2) students may opt out of funding an objectionable group only if the state university does not distribute its money in a viewpoint neutral manner.

UNBRIDLED DISCRETION AND VIEWPOINT NEUTRALITY

Courts increasingly interpret the obligation of viewpoint neutrality to require state colleges and universities to do two things to ensure that they do not act unconstitutionally. First, they must set forth clear, objective, and non-ideological standards that all applicants must meet to receive funding. Without such standards, recent court decisions have held, colleges and universities may not compel all students to contribute funds that are disbursed to student groups. That was the holding of the U.S. Court of Appeals for the Seventh Circuit, in its potentially pathbreaking decision in *Southworth v. Board of Regents of the University of Wisconsin System* (2002), when it applied the Supreme Court's 2000 decision to the facts of the case at the University of Wisconsin. Vague standards are unconstitutional, the court held, because they would enable the government to make decisions about whether to fund student groups according to the ideological, political, religious, or other preferences of the government officials. In this case, "the government" is university officials or their agents (such as student governments or committees). The Supreme Court has a wonderful term for this unconstitutional practice of governing people by vague rules: "unbridled discretion." If a state university uses such arbitrary power and procedures to distribute money, then it cannot constitutionally require students to pay the fee. There are several safeguards against the danger of forbidden unbridled discretion. A public campus, in distributing student fees, must state and follow a clear policy that prohibits making funding decisions on the basis of a group's viewpoint. It must require student government (or other) officials to give written reasons why they are denying a grant. It must provide a fair and effective appeals process for those denied funding. Crucially, it must state nonideological standards that spell out very clearly what qualifications an applicant must meet to receive funding. Specific funding schemes may require additional safeguards to protect both student applicants and student contributors from funding based on the decision-makers' unbridled discretion. Such safeguards might include objective standards that remove discretion from student government leaders, requirements to put in writing the specific reasons for denying funding to a group, a right of appeal to nonstudent and impartial administrators, and similar barriers against arbitrary action.

FEES AND FUNDING AT PRIVATE COLLEGES AND UNIVERSITIES:
A Question of Contract

Private universities and colleges stand in a different relation to the Constitution than governmental institutions such as public universities and colleges. The Constitution limits only government action. Because a private college or university is not a governmental entity, it does not have to obey the First Amendment. Voluntary associations in the private society are a vital part of American freedom. The fact that a private institution is not bound by the Constitution, however, does not mean that it is not bound by the rule of law. Many private schools choose by their own formal and advertised policies to hold themselves to certain standards regarding freedom of speech, due process, diversity of opinion, academic freedom, and the protection of individual conscience. A private school that claims to adhere to such policies may be required under state laws that apply to contract or fraud to live up to its own internal standards—in this case, the protection of freedom of speech. Such policies might compel a private college or university to distribute student fees in a viewpoint neutral manner or prevent it from ordering a controversial student group to disband because the school objects to the views expressed by the group. The law does not permit breach of contract or fraud. This model might apply to private universities and colleges that promote no distinct ideological or religious belief system, or, above all, that promise certain standards of nondiscrimination, legal equality, and academic freedom. An institution that induces students to attend by promising legal equality, variety of viewpoints, and nondiscrimination may not break those promises with impunity.

By contrast, if a private college or university is organized around a specific set of ideological or political beliefs, then the First Amendment protects its right to require students to fund speech that promotes the beliefs of the college. Students attending a private school established around a clear system of belief have no legal right to demand that the school allow dissenters to express conflicting views on campus. The First Amendment's right of association protects the right of those private schools to promote their specific ideological or religious beliefs. A private college or university may not in good faith present itself as a secular liberal arts institution that guarantees a student's right to free expression but then, in practice, further a particular ideological or religious agenda by funding only organizations that promote that agenda. Such a practice would arguably violate the contractual obligation that the institution has undertaken to the student to whom it has promised a liberal arts education in a setting in which the free marketplace of ideas prevails. (When a vendor advertises one product but then offers a different one in its place, that is known as "bait and switch." When a vendor claims to sell you one product but secretly substitutes another, that act is known as "fraud.")

FREQUENTLY ASKED QUESTIONS

Because the law involving mandatory student fees has been expounded almost exclusively in the realm of public colleges and universities, most of these questions are posed only in that context. Private colleges and universities that claim or wish to extend to their students the same rights that public colleges and universities *must* extend under the Constitution should adopt the same policies. That is a vital moral issue. The Bill of Rights limits the power of government over free individuals and groups. It also reflects moral values that are desirable ends in themselves. If a private college or university is going to extend fewer rights and protections to its students than a public institution constitutionally must extend, it certainly should make that fact clear to applicants, students, and donors.

My public university functions as if mandatory student fees were the only way to fund campus organizations. May a public university or college choose to fund campus organizations with funds other than those exacted by a mandatory student fee?

Yes, most definitely. Students are not the only source of funding for campus organizations. Universities that desire to foster expression of diverse views on campus may choose to stimulate debate by funding controversial campus organizations in a variety of ways. Universities may seek voluntary contributions from alumni, foundations, corporations, labor unions, the general public, and individual students themselves. Student organizations are also free to apply to such outside sources, and may well find that they learn valuable lessons about the "real world" if they have to convince people to contribute voluntarily to them. Also, public universities and colleges can avoid the moral and legal problems that come with requiring students to pay funds to groups they find objectionable by obtaining funding from alternative sources and making payment of the student activities fee optional.

May a college allow students to opt out of funding groups that they find objectionable?

Yes. A college or university is free to recognize the rights of conscience of individual students, allowing them to opt out of funding groups that these students find objectionable. This can be done administratively without a lawsuit or court order. For example, the University of Minnesota has established a procedure for students to receive refunds of their funding of MPIRG (Minnesota Public Interest Research Group). Institutions of higher learning would be respecting the highest principles by not forcing unwilling students to fund groups they find objectionable. On the other hand, there are those who argue, with some force, that because the function of a liberal arts university is to promote the free marketplace of ideas, a large number and variety of student-funded organizations contribute to the intellectual diversity on the campus. In this way, they argue, the imposition on students to fund organizations whose ideological agendas they disagree with is a minimal intrusion, as long as funding is distributed in a viewpoint neutral manner. The argument, in short, is that students of the widest possible diversity of beliefs benefit from having both their own and others' views represented among campus organizations. This question—whether it is better to deny all mandatory funding or to allow mandatory funding in a viewpoint neutral manner—is a personal and philosophical one on which reasonable people may disagree. However, the Supreme Court has spoken, and it has insisted that if public colleges and universities choose mandatory funding, they must follow a policy of viewpoint neutrality.

At my public university, we decide to fund campus organizations through a referendum. Is that constitutional?

No. In *Southworth*, the Supreme Court ruled that referenda to decide funding would almost certainly violate the principle of viewpoint neutrality. If a power oversteps constitutional limits, it does not matter whether it is a minority or a majority that exercises that power. A referendum invites a majority of voting students to violate viewpoint neutrality. Referenda offer no protection from the tyranny of the majority in matters of mandatory fees and the allocation of funding. State universities may not force students to fund groups that win funding through a referendum, nor may they deny a group funding solely because it does not receive sufficient support in a referendum.

My public college forces me to contribute to the local PIRG, and the PIRG then claims that I am a member because of my compelled contribution. Is that constitutional?

No. A state university cannot compel you to "join" a private organization that advocates ideas you oppose as a condition of attending and graduating from that institution. Although a university is able to compel funding of such a group if it is funded through a viewpoint neutral process, the university violates the Constitution if it allows the funded organization to count all of the compelled contributors as "members" of the organization. Such a requirement violates an individual's rights of conscience and association, because membership indicates that the individual voluntarily chose to join the group. The university might fund a pro-life and a pro-choice student group; it may not compel you to be a member of either.

At my state university, an official policy prohibits funding of student organizations that are "religious or politically partisan." Is that unconstitutional viewpoint discrimination?

Yes. A formal policy excluding campus organizations from receiving funding because of the views they advocate is a classic form of viewpoint discrimination and was found unconstitutional by the United States Supreme Court in *Rosenberger*. No campus organization may be categorically denied funding by university policy because of the views it espouses. Further, a state university may not create restrictions on funding for some groups, based on the viewpoints they advocate, while not similarly restricting groups that espouse other ideas. Legal equality among viewpoints is the rule of thumb here. For example, it is unconstitutional to prohibit religious and political groups from using their grants to fund guest speakers while allowing other campus groups to do so. The golden rule applies here.

Is it constitutional for my public college or university to prohibit student groups from receiving funding or meeting on campus unless they sign a statement pledging not to discriminate?

This is an area of law that is only now being explored by the courts, but certain aspects of this issue seem clear. First, if student organizations are private, voluntary groups, state universities and colleges might well be violating the students' freedom of association by requiring such groups to sign antidiscrimination statements. It would be unconstitutional, for example, for a state university to require a student organization to accept members or leaders who disagree with the basic tenets of the organization. The campus vegetarians could not be compelled to have butchers and hunters join their ranks, or the campus gay group to allow students who oppose homosexuality. The libertarians could not be kicked off campus because they refuse to allow communists to become members (or vice-versa). If such groups could not organize around their common beliefs and purposes, there could be no organizations devoted to those beliefs and purposes. However, a university could probably require that the ski club or chess club not discriminate on the basis of race or religion, because the prohibited categories do not infringe on the purpose that caused the organizers to form the private group. A university nondiscrimination policy raises significant and obvious First Amendment concerns when it would violate the organization's rights to freedom of speech, association, and the free exercise of religion. For example, a Jewish, Christian, Muslim, or atheist organization on campus should be permitted to require that its leaders be, respectively, Jewish, Christian, Muslim, or atheistic, because Judaism, Christianity, Islam, or atheism is the set of ideas around which each group formed. To force a religious antidiscrimination rule on a religious group would eliminate most religious groups' foundational beliefs, imposing on all faiths the religious view of the group that believed that "all roads lead to God." If controversial, even despised groups may not express their views in the marketplace of ideas found on a university campus, then freedom of expression is in serious jeopardy.

Are you saying, then, that colleges and universities must tolerate "discriminatory groups" on campus?
The central problem here is that a practice that a college or university might deem "discrimination" is, to a student group, necessary to preserve the group's identity. A case involving that question arose recently at Tufts University, a private institution. The student government denied funding (and recognition) to the Tufts Christian Fellowship (TCF) for refusing to promise an openly lesbian member who believed that Scripture held a favorable view of homosexuality that it would not take her views into account when considering her for a leadership position. In Tufts' initial view, the TCF was guilty of dis-

crimination on the basis of sexual orientation. After many contentious hearings and considerable outside publicity, TCF prevailed on the ground that it would have violated the religious freedom of TCF's members if they were forced to accept a leader who openly espoused views that their chosen religion deemed sinful. Supporters of TCF asked if the campus Gay, Lesbian, Bisexual, and Transgendered Alliance would have to choose as a leader someone who believed that homosexuality was a sin. Tufts eventually understood that every group's freedom depends on the right of individuals to come together around a shared cause or purpose. Colleges and universities that trample, in the name of diversity, the right of organizations to form around a common nucleus of ideas end up by destroying all possibility of diversity.

How would I wage a successful campaign against non-viewpoint-neutral funding at my public university?
One way to protect funding decisions from ideological abuse is for the university to spell out clear, neutral, non-ideological standards as the sole conditions for receiving funding. As noted earlier, in the second *Southworth* decision (2002), the U.S. Court of Appeals for the Seventh Circuit ruled that the U.S. Constitution requires state universities to spell out clear standards in order to restrain the unbridled discretion of student government

officials to fund or defund groups according to their
ideological viewpoints. If an applicant meets those standards, the group would be entitled to funding. This limits the discretion of the student government or officials
who allocate the money and ensures that they do not bias
their funding decisions based on their ideological agendas (which could change, of course, over time). Colleges
and universities have convinced the Supreme Court that
compulsory systems are justified because they enlarge
the range of opinions to which students are exposed and
thus enhance the college's educational mission. That is
so, however, the Court ruled, only if viewpoint neutrality prevails. A public college or university cannot impose
or use mandatory fees to create a system in which students at one end of the political or religious spectrum are
forced to fund ideas with which they disagree while
never allowing them to fund ideas with which they agree.
That would be a fair rule, as well, for private colleges or
universities that do not advertise a particular religious or
secular sectarian mission. Under the system approved by
the Supreme Court, any student organization would be
entitled to funding if it met specific and objective non-
ideological standards. Recall also, and use to your right-
ful advantage, that in the case of *Southworth v. Board of
Regents of the University of Wisconsin System* (2002), the
Court insisted that a truly neutral system would also
deny the unbridled discretion to make funding decisions

to student government members or school officials. A system that passed constitutional scrutiny would forbid policies that deny funding to groups simply because of what they advocate. It would not allow viewpoint to form any part of a policy placing limits on a group's ability to seek funding. These rules also should apply at private institutions that wish to enjoy the same range of protections from arbitrary power. Urge officials at your school to adopt a policy that allows dissenting students to opt out of funding groups of which they disapprove. Also urge university officials to seek other sources of funding for student organizations (alumni, foundations, corporations, and so on), freeing unwilling students from being compelled to fund groups that they find objectionable.

How should I respond when my public university or college claims that it is under no obligation to fund my worthwhile cause?

The stated goal of mandatory fee systems is to fund a wide spectrum of viewpoints and voices on campus. If a group meets reasonable and neutral criteria—for example, that it have at least five members, that all its members be students, that it meet on campus at least once a month during the school year—then the group would be automatically entitled to a set amount of funding, possibly based on how many students are members. If a university is "under no obligation" to fund a particular group, then that university should not be allowed to force unwilling students to fund the groups the university does choose to fund. Otherwise, a university could pick and choose which groups receive money, favoring viewpoints it supports and denying funding to ideas it does not like. Most campus organizations, in fact, do not receive funding from mandatory student fees. For example, during the 1995-96 academic year at the University of Wisconsin, at the height of the *Southworth* litigation, only 183 of the 623 registered student groups on campus (29%) received money collected from the mandatory student fee. During the 1990-91 academic year at the University of Virginia, while the *Rosenberger* litigation was pending, only 118 out of a total of 343 student organizations (34%) received funding from the mandatory student fee. If a university funds only about one third of all student groups, this creates a great temptation to fund only the organizations whose views it favors. This danger is eliminated if all student groups can receive funding if they meet neutral and reasonable criteria.

What is the best way to request funding for my organization?
Follow every requirement, file every requested form, meet every deadline, and attend every hearing that you are supposed to attend. Student government members and university officials may be wary of funding a new

organization. Be prepared to apply several years in a row before you receive funding. However, if the student government at a public college or university consistently denies funding to a certain controversial group, that organization may consider contacting an attorney to look over the documents for a possible violation of the First Amendment.

When does too little funding constitute a repression of speech?

Unequal treatment—usually referred to in the law as "disparate treatment"—is the key here. If an organization is denied funding because it did not comply with obscure provisions of the application process, but the same requirements are waived for other groups, it is time to start asking questions about disparate treatment. The same principle is true in the case of inequalities in funding. If the funds from student fees flow primarily to liberal and leftist organizations, or to conservative and right-wing organizations, ask how that could be so. Does something in the funding procedure favor only certain ideological groups in terms of positive responses and amounts awarded? Apply two years in a row to see if a pattern of discrimination exists. Make certain that younger members of your organization receive and maintain the records of older and graduating members. If you can demonstrate that you have been the recipient of repeated questionable funding decisions, you will greatly strengthen your case. Many universities have mechanisms that allow student groups to appeal funding decisions. If you believe that the student government is refusing to fund your group because of your viewpoint, you can appeal through formal university channels. The process may or may not be stacked against denied applicants, or conservatives, or liberals, and so on. Overall, though, the appeals process may grant you quicker relief than going to court. Form coalitions with groups denied adequate funding on seemingly similar discriminatory grounds. Expose the abuses. Always remember and apply the profound saying of Supreme Court Justice Louis Brandeis: "Sunlight is the best disinfectant."

My organization applied for funding to counteract the advocacy of various politically activist groups on campus, but the student government and the University denied my funding request because my group does not offer a "service" to students. Is this permitted?

Funding mischief often occurs when student governments fund "student services." Some universities will fund the overhead expenses of campus groups, but others will give large amounts of money to other groups to provide what are defined as "services" for students. Sometimes, these services are legitimately defined.

Examples of legitimate services include shuttle bus services, study support centers, rape trauma response programs, and so on. However, some universities have defined lobbying and political or ideological advocacy for a specific viewpoint to be a "service" that all students should be required to fund. Between 2000 and 2001, for example, the University of Wisconsin gave approximately $75,000 to WISPIRG to support its "service" of lobbying the Wisconsin Legislature and advocating its generally liberal viewpoints on campus. When the student government funds advocates of only one side of a debate and deems this advocacy a service to all students, then presumably those advocating contrary viewpoints are performing a "disservice." To say the very least, that is not constitutionally required viewpoint neutrality. This is how a system of mandatory student fees, however, too often ends up funding groups from one side of a debate and not the other. When the University of Wisconsin gives $50,000 a year to a campus gay organization to promote tolerance and acceptance of homosexuals, is it paying for a service that students in general can use, or is it amplifying the voice of one side of a controversial debate? Would the student government also give $50,000 to a group of "ex-gays" offering to help homosexuals who wished to change their sexual orientation? To prevent such abuses, students should work for a definition of "student services" that does not define advocacy as a service and that identifies things that truly benefit all or most students. Partisan lobbying and advocacy may be of truly great value to this or that cause, but they are not "student services."

My environmentally sensitive state university uses mandatory fee money to fund a shuttle bus service and a recycling center for aluminum cans. I think that these are boondoggles, part of an environmentalist political cause, a waste of my money, and a subsidy of people with whom I disagree. Since the university does not fund a "gas guzzler" shuttle system or a throw-away aluminum can service, isn't it engaging in viewpoint discrimination? May I therefore opt out of funding them?

No. First Amendment protections for students only apply when the university is funding advocacy. The university is free to fund things that do not advocate ideas, and it is free to force unwilling students to fund them. Shuttle services and recycling centers do not advocate viewpoints but, rather, reflect public policy choices. The fact that a student thinks the shuttle service or the aluminum can recycling center are boondoggles does not mean he or she can opt out of funding them. What that student can do, however, is run for student government and work through the political process to defund what he or she sees as "boondoggles."

A professor at the state university I attend teaches a class in which he voices support for scientific creationism and traditional marriage. Another professor advocates Darwinism and the breakdown of the traditional family. May students who object to those viewpoints opt out of paying the portion of their tuition that provides the salaries of those professors? No. Classroom situations are very different from the mandatory student fee situation. Tuition helps fund the educational program of a state university, so a professor is part of that educational system. Students who desire a degree from the state university cannot disrupt the official program established by the state. By contrast, campus organizations receiving mandatory student fees are neither controlled by nor affiliated with the government. Therefore, a state university can compel a student to fund a professor in the biology department whom that student finds objectionable, because the student seeks a degree from the university and the professor is part of the university's formal educational process. However, a private campus organization operated independently of university control is quite different.

CONCLUSION

Know and defend your constitutional and moral rights at public colleges and universities, and your moral and contractual rights at private colleges and universities. These issues are not simply topics of constitutional law. They are the stuff of liberty, legal equality, freedom of association, human dignity, and a free society.

APPENDIX:
The Crucial Court Opinions
on Student Fees

I. *Board of Regents of the University of Wisconsin System v. Southworth*, 529 U.S. 217 (2000).

Majority Opinion

JUSTICE KENNEDY delivered the opinion of the Court.

For the second time in recent years we consider constitutional questions arising from a program designed to facilitate extracurricular student speech at a public university. Respondents are a group of students at the University of Wisconsin. They brought a First Amendment challenge to a mandatory student activity fee imposed by petitioner Board of Regents of the University of Wisconsin and used in part by the University to support student organizations engaging in political or ideological speech. Respondents object to the speech and expression of some of the student organizations. Relying upon our precedents which protect members of unions and bar associations from being required to pay fees used for speech the members find objectionable, both the District Court and the Court of Appeals invalidated the University's student fee program. The University contends that its mandatory student activity fee and the speech which it supports are appropriate to further its educational mission.

We reverse. The First Amendment permits a public university to charge its students an activity fee used to fund a program to facilitate extracurricular student speech if the program is viewpoint neutral. We do not sustain, however, the student referendum mechanism of the University's program, which appears to permit the exaction of fees in violation of the viewpoint neutrality principle. As to that aspect of the program, we remand for further proceedings.

I

The University of Wisconsin is a public corporation of the State of Wisconsin. See Wis. Stat. § 36.07(1) (1993-1994). State law defines the University's mission in broad terms: "to develop human resources, to discover and disseminate knowledge, to extend knowledge and its application beyond the boundaries of its campuses and to serve and stimulate society by developing in students heightened intellectual, cultural and humane sensitivities . . . and a sense of purpose." § 36.01(2). Some 30,000 undergraduate students and 10,000 graduate and professional students attend the University's Madison campus, ranking it among the Nation's largest institutions of higher learning. Students come to the renowned University from all 50 States and from 72 foreign countries. Last year marked its 150th anniversary, and to celebrate its distinguished history, the University sponsored a series of research initiatives, campus forums and workshops, historical exhibits, and public lectures, all reaffirming its commitment to explore the universe of knowledge and ideas.

The responsibility for governing the University of Wisconsin System is vested by law with the board of regents. § 36.09(1). The same law empowers the students to share in aspects of the University's governance. One of those functions is to administer the student activities fee program. By statute the "students in consultation with the chancellor and subject to the final confirmation of the board [of regents] shall have the responsibility for the disposition of those student fees which constitute substantial support for campus student activities." § 36.09(5). The students do so, in large measure, through their student government, called the Associated Students of Madison (ASM), and various ASM subcommittees. The program the University maintains to support the extracurricular activities undertaken by many of its student organizations is the subject of the present controversy.

It seems that since its founding the University has required full-time students enrolled at its Madison campus to pay a nonrefundable activity fee. App. 154. For the 1995-1996 academic year, when this suit was commenced, the activity fee amounted to $331.50 per year. The fee is segregated from the University's tuition charge. Once collected, the activity fees are deposited by the University into the accounts of the State of Wisconsin. Id. at 9. The fees are drawn upon by the University to support various campus services and extracurricular student activities. In the University's view, the activity fees "enhance the educational experience" of its students by "promoting extracurricular activities," "stimulating advocacy and debate on diverse points of view," enabling "participation in political activity," "promoting student participation in campus administrative activity," and providing "opportunities to develop social skills," all consistent with the University's mission. Id. at 154-155.

The board of regents classifies the segregated fee into allocable and nonallocable portions. The nonallocable portion approximates 80% of the total fee and covers expenses such as student health services, intramural sports, debt service, and the upkeep and operations of the student union facilities. Id. at 13. Respondents did not challenge the purposes to which the University commits the nonallocable portion of the segregated fee. Id. at 37.

The allocable portion of the fee supports extracurricular endeavors pursued by the University's registered student organizations or RSO's. To qualify for RSO status, students must organize as a not-for-profit group, limit membership primarily to students, and agree to undertake activities related to student life on campus. Id. at 15. During the 1995-1996 school year, 623 groups had RSO status on the Madison campus. Id. at 255. To name but a few, RSO's included the Future Financial Gurus of America; the International Socialist Organization; the College Democrats; the College Republicans; and the American Civil Liberties Union Campus Chapter. As one would expect, the expressive activities undertaken by RSO's are diverse in range and content, from displaying posters and circulating newsletters throughout the campus, to hosting campus debates and guest speakers, and to what can best be described as political lobbying.

RSO's may obtain a portion of the allocable fees in one of three ways. Most do so by seeking funding from the Student Government Activity Fund (SGAF), administered by the ASM. SGAF moneys may be issued to support an RSO's operations and events, as well as travel expenses "central to the purpose of the organization." Id. at 18. As an alternative, an RSO can apply for funding from the General Student Services Fund (GSSF), administered through the ASM's finance committee. During the 1995-1996 academic year, 15 RSO's received GSSF funding. These RSO's included a campus tutoring center, the student radio station, a student environmental group, a gay and bisexual student center, a community legal office, an AIDS support network, a campus women's center, and the Wisconsin Student Public Interest Research Group (WISPIRG). Id. at 16-17. The University acknowledges that, in addition to providing campus services (e.g., tutoring and counseling), the GSSF-funded RSO's engage in political and ideological expression. Brief for Petitioner 10.

The GSSF, as well as the SGAF, consists of moneys originating in the allocable portion of the mandatory fee. The parties have stipulated that, with respect to SGAF and GSSF funding, "the process for reviewing and approving allocations for funding is administered in a viewpoint-neutral fashion," Id. at 14-15, and that the University does not use the fee program for "advocating a particular point of view," Id. at 39.

A student referendum provides a third means for an RSO to obtain funding. Id. at 16. While the record is sparse on this feature of the University's program, the parties inform us that the student body can vote either to approve or to disapprove an assessment for a particular RSO. One referendum resulted in an allocation of $45,000 to WISPIRG during the 1995-1996 academic year. At oral argument, counsel for the University acknowledged that a referendum could also operate to defund an RSO or to veto a funding decision of the ASM. In October 1996, for example, the student body voted to terminate funding to a national student organization to which the University belonged. Id. at 215. Both parties confirmed at oral argument that their stipulation regarding the program's viewpoint neutrality does not extend to the referendum process. Tr. of Oral Arg. 19, 29.

With respect to GSSF and SGAF funding, the ASM or its finance committee makes initial funding decisions. App. 14-15. The ASM does so in an open session, and interested students may attend meetings when RSO funding is discussed. Id. at 14. It also appears that the ASM must approve the results of a student referendum. Approval appears pro forma, however, as counsel for the University advised us that the student government "voluntarily views the referendum as binding." Tr. of Oral Arg. 15. Once the ASM approves an RSO's funding application, it forwards its decision to the chancellor and to the board of regents for their review and approval. App. 18, 19. Approximately 30% of the University's RSO's received funding during the 1995-1996 academic year.

RSO's, as a general rule, do not receive lump-sum cash distributions. Rather, RSO's obtain funding support on a reimbursement basis by submitting receipts or invoices to the University. Guidelines identify expenses appropriate for reimbursement. Permitted expenditures include, in the main, costs for printing, postage, office supplies, and use of University facilities and equipment. Materials printed with student fees must contain a disclaimer that the views expressed are not those of the ASM. The University also reimburses RSO's for fees arising from membership in "other related and non-profit organizations." Id. at 251.

The University's policy establishes purposes for which fees may not be expended. RSO's may not receive reimbursement for "gifts, donations, and contributions," the costs of legal services, or for "activities which are politically partisan or religious in nature." Id. at 251-252. (The policy does not give examples of the prohibited expenditures.) A separate policy statement on GSSF funding states that an RSO can receive funding if it "does not have a primarily political orientation (i.e. is not a registered political group)." Id. at 238. The same policy adds that an RSO "shall not use [student fees] for any lobbying purposes." Ibid. At one point in their brief respondents suggest that the prohibition against expenditures for "politically partisan" purposes renders the program not viewpoint neutral. Brief for Respondents 31. In view of the fact that both parties entered a stipulation to the contrary at the outset of this litigation, which was again reiterated during oral argument in this Court, we do not consider respondents' challenge to this aspect of the University's program.

The University's Student Organization Handbook has guidelines for regulating the conduct and activities of RSO's. In addition to obligating RSO's to adhere to the fee program's rules and regulations, the guidelines establish procedures authorizing any student to complain to the University that an RSO is in noncompliance. An extensive investigative process is in place to evaluate and remedy violations. The University's policy includes a range of sanctions for noncompliance, including probation, suspension, or termination of RSO status.

One RSO that appears to operate in a manner distinct from others is WISPIRG. For reasons not clear from the record, WISPIRG receives lump-sum cash distributions from the University. University counsel informed us that this distribution reduced the GSSF portion of the fee pool. Tr. of Oral Arg. 15. The full extent of the uses to which WISPIRG puts its funds is unclear. We do know, however, that WISPIRG sponsored on-campus events regarding homelessness and environmental and consumer protection issues. App. 348. It coordinated community food drives and educational programs and spent a portion of its activity fees for the lobbying efforts of its parent organization and for student internships aimed at influencing legislation. Id. at 344, 347.

In March 1996, respondents, each of whom attended or still attend the University's Madison campus, filed suit in the United States District Court for the Western District of Wisconsin against members of the board of regents. Respondents alleged, inter alia, that imposition of the segregated fee violated their rights of free speech, free association, and free exercise under the First Amendment. They contended the University must grant them the choice not to fund those RSO's that engage in political and ideological expression offensive to their personal beliefs. Respondents requested both injunctive and declaratory relief. On cross-motions for summary judgment, the District Court ruled in their favor, declaring the University's segregated fee program invalid under Abood v. Detroit Bd. of Ed., 431 U.S. 209, 52 L. Ed. 2d 261, 97 S. Ct. 1782 (1977), and Keller v. State Bar of Cal., 496 U.S. 1, 110 L. Ed. 2d 1, 110 S. Ct. 2228 (1990). The District Court decided the fee program compelled students "to support political and ideological activity with which they disagree" in violation of respondents' First Amendment rights to freedom of speech and association. App. to Pet for Cert. 98a. The court did not reach respondents' free exercise claim. The District Court's order enjoined the board of regents from using segregated fees to fund any RSO engaging in political or ideological speech.

The United States Court of Appeals for the Seventh Circuit affirmed in part, reversed in part, and vacated in part. Southworth v. Grebe, 151 F.3d 717 (1998). As the District Court had done, the Court of Appeals found our compelled speech precedents controlling. After examining the University's fee program under the three-part test outlined in Lehnert v. Ferris Faculty Assn., 500 U.S. 507, 114 L. Ed. 2d 572, 111 S. Ct. 1950 (1991), it concluded that the program was not germane to the University's mission, did not further a vital policy of the

University, and imposed too much of a burden on respondents' free speech rights. "Like the objecting union members in Abood," the Court of Appeals reasoned, the students here have a First Amendment interest in not being compelled to contribute to an organization whose expressive activities conflict with their own personal beliefs. 151 F.3d at 731. It added that protecting the objecting students' free speech rights was "of heightened concern" following our decision in Rosenberger v. Rector and Visitors of Univ. of Va., 515 U.S. 819, 132 L. Ed. 2d 700, 115 S. Ct. 2510 (1995), because "if the university cannot discriminate in the disbursement of funds, it is imperative that students not be compelled to fund organizations which engage in political and ideological activities—that is the only way to protect the individual's rights." 151 F.3d at 730, n. 11. The Court of Appeals extended the District Court's order and enjoined the board of regents from requiring objecting students to pay that portion of the fee used to fund RSO's engaged in political or ideological expression. 151 F.3d at 735.

Three members of the Court of Appeals dissented from the denial of the University's motion for rehearing en banc. In their view, the panel opinion overlooked the "crucial difference between a requirement to pay money to an organization that explicitly aims to subsidize one viewpoint to the exclusion of other viewpoints, as in Abood and Keller, and a requirement to pay a fee to a group that creates a viewpoint-neutral forum, as is true of the student activity fee here." Southworth v. Grebe, 157 F.3d 1124, 1129 (CA7 1998) (D. Wood, J., dissenting).

Other courts addressing First Amendment challenges to similar student fee programs have reached conflicting results. Compare Rounds v. Oregon State Bd. of Higher Ed., 166 F.3d 1032, 1038-1040 (CA9 1999), Hays County Guardian v. Supple, 969 F.2d 111, 123 (CA5 1992), cert. denied, 506 U.S. 1087, 122 L. Ed. 2d 371, 113 S. Ct. 1067 (1993), Kania v. Fordham, 702 F.2d 475, 480 (CA4 1983), Good v. Associated Students of Univ. of Wash., 86 Wn.2d 94, 105, 542 P.2d 762, 769 (1975) (en banc), with Smith v. Regents of Univ. of Cal., 4 Cal. 4th 843, 862-863, 844 P.2d 500, 513-514 cert. denied, 510 U.S. 863, 126 L. Ed. 2d 140, 114 S. Ct. 181 (1993). These conflicts, together with the importance of the issue presented, led us to grant certiorari. 526 U.S. 1038, 119 S. Ct. 1332, 143 L. Ed. 2d 497 (1999). We reverse the judgment of the Court of Appeals.

II

It is inevitable that government will adopt and pursue programs and policies within its constitutional powers but which nevertheless are contrary to the profound beliefs and sincere convictions of some of its citizens. The government, as a general rule, may support valid programs and policies by taxes or other exactions binding on protesting parties. Within this broader principle it seems inevitable that funds raised by the government will be spent for speech and other expression to advocate and defend its own policies. See, e.g., Rust v. Sullivan, 500 U.S. 173, 114 L. Ed. 2d 233, 111 S. Ct. 1759 (1991); Regan v. Taxation With Representation of Wash., 461 U.S. 540, 548-549, 76 L. Ed. 2d 129, 103 S. Ct. 1997 (1983). The case we decide here, however, does not raise the issue of the government's right, or, to be more specific, the state-controlled University's right, to use its own funds to advance a particular message. The University's whole justification for fostering the challenged expression is that it springs from the initiative of the students, who alone give it purpose and content in the course of their extracurricular endeavors.

The University having disclaimed that the speech is its own, we do not reach the question whether traditional political controls to ensure responsible government action would be sufficient to overcome First Amendment objections and to allow the challenged program under the principle that the government can speak for itself. If the challenged speech here were financed by tuition dollars and the University and its officials were responsible for its content, the case might be evaluated on the premise that the government itself is the speaker. That is not the case before us.

The University of Wisconsin exacts the fee at issue for

the sole purpose of facilitating the free and open exchange of ideas by, and among, its students. We conclude the objecting students may insist upon certain safeguards with respect to the expressive activities which they are required to support. Our public forum cases are instructive here by close analogy. This is true even though the student activities fund is not a public forum in the traditional sense of the term and despite the circumstance that those cases most often involve a demand for access, not a claim to be exempt from supporting speech. See, e.g., Lamb's Chapel v. Center Moriches Union Free School Dist., 508 U.S. 384, 124 L. Ed. 2d 352, 113 S. Ct. 2141 (1993); Widmar v. Vincent, 454 U.S. 263, 70 L. Ed. 2d 440, 102 S. Ct. 269 (1981). The standard of viewpoint neutrality found in the public forum cases provides the standard we find controlling. We decide that the viewpoint neutrality requirement of the University program is in general sufficient to protect the rights of the objecting students. The student referendum aspect of the program for funding speech and expressive activities, however, appears to be inconsistent with the viewpoint neutrality requirement.

We must begin by recognizing that the complaining students are being required to pay fees which are subsidies for speech they find objectionable, even offensive. The Abood and Keller cases, then, provide the beginning point for our analysis. Abood v. Detroit Bd. of Ed., 431 U.S. 209, 52 L. Ed. 2d 261, 97 S. Ct. 1782 (1977);

Keller v. State Bar of Cal., 496 U.S. 1, 110 L. Ed. 2d 1, 110 S. Ct. 2228 (1990). While those precedents identify the interests of the protesting students, the means of implementing First Amendment protections adopted in those decisions are neither applicable nor workable in the context of extracurricular student speech at a university.

In Abood, some nonunion public school teachers challenged an agreement requiring them, as a condition of their employment, to pay a service fee equal in amount to union dues. 431 U.S. at 211-212. The objecting teachers alleged that the union's use of their fees to engage in political speech violated their freedom of association guaranteed by the First and Fourteenth Amendments. Id. at 213. The Court agreed and held that any objecting teacher could "prevent the Union's spending a part of their required service fees to contribute to political candidates and to express political views unrelated to its duties as exclusive bargaining representative." 431 U.S. at 234. The principles outlined in Abood provided the foundation for our later decision in Keller. There we held that lawyers admitted to practice in California could be required to join a state bar association and to fund activities "germane" to the association's mission of "regulating the legal profession and improving the quality of legal services." 496 U.S. at 13-14. The lawyers could not, however, be required to fund the bar association's own political expression. Id. at 16.

The proposition that students who attend the University cannot be required to pay subsidies for the speech of other students without some First Amendment protection follows from the Abood and Keller cases. Students enroll in public universities to seek fulfillment of their personal aspirations and of their own potential. If the University conditions the opportunity to receive a college education, an opportunity comparable in importance to joining a labor union or bar association, on an agreement to support objectionable, extracurricular expression by other students, the rights acknowledged in Abood and Keller become implicated. It infringes on the speech and beliefs of the individual to be required, by this mandatory student activity fee program, to pay subsidies for the objectionable speech of others without any recognition of the State's corresponding duty to him or her. Yet recognition must be given as well to the important and substantial purposes of the University, which seeks to facilitate a wide range of speech.

In Abood and Keller the constitutional rule took the form of limiting the required subsidy to speech germane to the purposes of the union or bar association. The standard of germane speech as applied to student speech at a university is unworkable, however, and gives insufficient protection both to the objecting students and to the University program itself. Even in the context of a labor union, whose functions are, or so we might have thought, well known and understood by the law and the courts after a long history of government regulation and judicial involvement, we have encountered difficulties in deciding what is germane and what is not. The difficulty manifested itself in our decision in Lehnert v. Ferris Faculty Assn., 500 U.S. 507, 114 L. Ed. 2d 572, 111 S. Ct. 1950 (1991), where different members of the Court reached varying conclusions regarding what expressive activity was or was not germane to the mission of the association. If it is difficult to define germane speech with ease or precision where a union or bar association is the party, the standard becomes all the more unmanageable in the public university setting, particularly where the State undertakes to stimulate the whole universe of speech and ideas.

The speech the University seeks to encourage in the program before us is distinguished not by discernable limits but by its vast, unexplored bounds. To insist upon asking what speech is germane would be contrary to the very goal the University seeks to pursue. It is not for the Court to say what is or is not germane to the ideas to be pursued in an institution of higher learning.

Just as the vast extent of permitted expression makes the test of germane speech inappropriate for intervention, so too does it underscore the high potential for intrusion on the First Amendment rights of the objecting students. It is all but inevitable that the fees will result in subsidies to speech which some students find objectionable and offensive to their personal beliefs. If the standard of germane speech is inapplicable, then, it might be argued the remedy is to allow each student to list those causes which he or she will or will not support. If a university decided that its students' First Amendment interests were better protected by some type of optional or refund system it would be free to do so. We decline to impose a system of that sort as a constitutional requirement, however. The restriction could be so disruptive and expensive that the program to support extracurricular speech would be ineffective. The First Amendment does not require the University to put the program at risk.

The University may determine that its mission is well served if students have the means to engage in dynamic discussions of philosophical, religious, scientific, social, and political subjects in their extracurricular campus life outside the lecture hall. If the University reaches this conclusion, it is entitled to impose a mandatory fee to sustain an open dialogue to these ends.

The University must provide some protection to its students' First Amendment interests, however. The proper measure, and the principal standard of protection for objecting students, we conclude, is the requirement of viewpoint neutrality in the allocation of funding support. Viewpoint neutrality was the obligation to which we gave substance in Rosenberger v. Rector and Visitors of Univ. of Va., 515 U.S. 819, 132 L. Ed. 2d 700, 115 S.

Ct. 2510 (1995). There the University of Virginia feared that any association with a student newspaper advancing religious viewpoints would violate the Establishment Clause. We rejected the argument, holding that the school's adherence to a rule of viewpoint neutrality in administering its student fee program would prevent "any mistaken impression that the student newspapers speak for the University." Id. at 841. While Rosenberger was concerned with the rights a student has to use an extracurricular speech program already in place, today's case considers the antecedent question, acknowledged but unresolved in Rosenberger: whether a public university may require its students to pay a fee which creates the mechanism for the extracurricular speech in the first instance. When a university requires its students to pay fees to support the extracurricular speech of other students, all in the interest of open discussion, it may not prefer some viewpoints to others. There is symmetry then in our holding here and in Rosenberger: Viewpoint neutrality is the justification for requiring the student to pay the fee in the first instance and for ensuring the integrity of the program's operation once the funds have been collected. We conclude that the University of Wisconsin may sustain the extracurricular dimensions of its programs by using mandatory student fees with viewpoint neutrality as the operational principle.

The parties have stipulated that the program the

University has developed to stimulate extracurricular student expression respects the principle of viewpoint neutrality. If the stipulation is to continue to control the case, the University's program in its basic structure must be found consistent with the First Amendment.

We make no distinction between campus activities and the off-campus expressive activities of objectionable RSO's. Those activities, respondents tell us, often bear no relationship to the University's reason for imposing the segregated fee in the first instance, to foster vibrant campus debate among students. If the University shares those concerns, it is free to enact viewpoint neutral rules restricting off-campus travel or other expenditures by RSO's, for it may create what is tantamount to a limited public forum if the principles of viewpoint neutrality are respected. Cf. 515 U.S. at 829-830. We find no principled way, however, to impose upon the University, as a constitutional matter, a requirement to adopt geographic or spatial restrictions as a condition for RSOs' entitlement to reimbursement. Universities possess significant interests in encouraging students to take advantage of the social, civic, cultural, and religious opportunities available in surrounding communities and throughout the country. Universities, like all of society, are finding that traditional conceptions of territorial boundaries are difficult to insist upon in an age marked by revolutionary changes in communications, information transfer, and the means of discourse. If the rule of viewpoint neutrality is respected, our holding affords the University latitude to adjust its extracurricular student speech program to accommodate these advances and opportunities.

Our decision ought not to be taken to imply that in other instances the University, its agents or employees, or—of particular importance—its faculty, are subject to the First Amendment analysis which controls in this case. Where the University speaks, either in its own name through its regents or officers, or in myriad other ways through its diverse faculties, the analysis likely would be altogether different. See Rust v. Sullivan, 500 U.S. 173, 114 L. Ed. 2d 233, 111 S. Ct. 1759 (1991); Regan v. Taxation With Representation of Wash., 461 U.S. 540, 76 L. Ed. 2d 129, 103 S. Ct. 1997 (1983). The Court has not held, or suggested, that when the government speaks the rules we have discussed come into play.

When the government speaks, for instance to promote its own policies or to advance a particular idea, it is, in the end, accountable to the electorate and the political process for its advocacy. If the citizenry objects, newly elected officials later could espouse some different or contrary position. In the instant case, the speech is not that of the University or its agents. It is not, furthermore, speech by an instructor or a professor in the academic context, where principles applicable to government speech would have to be considered. Cf.

Rosenberger, supra, at 833 (discussing the discretion universities possess in deciding matters relating to their educational mission).

III

It remains to discuss the referendum aspect of the University's program. While the record is not well developed on the point, it appears that by majority vote of the student body a given RSO may be funded or defunded. It is unclear to us what protection, if any, there is for viewpoint neutrality in this part of the process. To the extent the referendum substitutes majority determinations for viewpoint neutrality it would undermine the constitutional protection the program requires. The whole theory of viewpoint neutrality is that minority views are treated with the same respect as are majority views. Access to a public forum, for instance, does not depend upon majoritarian consent. That principle is controlling here. A remand is necessary and appropriate to resolve this point; and the case in all events must be reexamined in light of the principles we have discussed. The judgment of the Court of Appeals is reversed, and the case is remanded for further proceedings consistent with this opinion. In this Court the parties shall bear their own costs.

It is so ordered.

II. *Rosenberger v. Rectors of the University of Virginia*, 515 U.S. 819 (1995).

Majority Opinion

JUSTICE KENNEDY delivered the opinion of the Court.

The University of Virginia, an instrumentality of the Commonwealth for which it is named and thus bound by the First and Fourteenth Amendments, authorizes the payment of outside contractors for the printing costs of a variety of student publications. It withheld any authorization for payments on behalf of petitioners for the sole reason that their student paper "primarily promotes or manifests a particular belief in or about a deity or an ultimate reality." That the paper did promote or manifest views within the defined exclusion seems plain enough. The challenge is to the University's regulation and its denial of authorization, the case raising issues under the Speech and Establishment Clauses of the First Amendment.

I

The public corporation we refer to as the "University" is denominated by state law as "the Rector and Visitors of the University of Virginia," Va. Code Ann. § 23-69 (1993), and it is responsible for governing the school, see § § 23-69 to 23-80. Founded by Thomas Jefferson in 1819, and ranked by him, together with the authorship of the Declaration of Independence and of the Virginia Act for Religious Freedom, Va. Code Ann. § 57-1 (1950), as one of his proudest achievements, the University is among the Nation's oldest and most respected seats of higher learning. It has more than 11,000 undergraduate students, and 6,000 graduate and professional students. An understanding of the case requires a somewhat detailed description of the program the University created to support extracurricular student activities on its campus.

Before a student group is eligible to submit bills from its outside contractors for payment by the fund described below, it must become a "Contracted Independent Organization" (CIO). CIO status is available to any group the majority of whose members are students, whose managing officers are full-time students, and that complies with certain procedural requirements. App. to Pet. for Cert. 2a. A CIO must file its constitution with the University; must pledge not to discriminate in its membership; and must include in dealings with third parties and in all written materials a disclaimer, stating that the CIO is independent of the University and that the University is not responsible for the CIO. App. 27-28. CIO's enjoy access to University facilities, including meeting rooms and computer terminals. Id., at 30. A standard agreement signed between each CIO and the University provides that the benefits and opportunities afforded to CIO's "should not be misinterpreted as meaning that those organizations are part of or controlled by the University, that the University is responsible for the organizations' contracts or other acts or omissions, or that the University approves of the organizations' goals or activities." Id., at 26.

All CIO's may exist and operate at the University, but some are also entitled to apply for funds from the Student Activities Fund (SAF). Established and governed by University Guidelines, the purpose of the SAF is to support a broad range of extracurricular student activities that "are related to the educational purpose of the University." App. to Pet. for Cert. 61a. The SAF is based on the University's "recognition that the availability of a wide range of opportunities" for its students "tends to enhance the University environment." App. 26. The Guidelines require that it be administered "in a manner consistent with the educational purpose of the University as well as with state and federal law." App. to Pet. for Cert. 61a. The SAF receives its money from a mandatory fee of $14 per semester assessed to each full-time student. The Student Council, elected by the students, has the initial authority to disburse the funds, but its actions are subject to review by a faculty body chaired by a designee of the Vice President for Student Affairs. Cf. id., at 63a-64a.

Some, but not all, CIO's may submit disbursement requests to the SAF. The Guidelines recognize 11 categories of student groups that may seek payment to third-party contractors because they "are related to the educational purpose of the University of Virginia." Id., at 61a-62a. One of these is "student news, information, opinion, entertainment, or academic communications media groups." Id., at 61a. The Guidelines also specify, however, that the costs of certain activities of CIO's that are otherwise eligible for funding will not be reimbursed by the SAF. The student activities that are excluded from SAF support are religious activities, philanthropic contributions and activities, political activities, activities that would jeopardize the University's tax-exempt status, those which involve payment of honoraria or similar fees, or social entertainment or related expenses. Id., at 62a-63a. The prohibition on "political activities" is defined so that it is limited to electioneering and lobbying. The Guidelines provide that "these restrictions on funding political activities are not intended to preclude funding of any otherwise eligible student organization which . . . espouses particular positions or ideological viewpoints, including those that may be unpopular or are not generally accepted." Id., at 65a-66a. A "religious activity," by contrast, is defined as any activity that "primarily promotes or manifests a particular belief in or about a deity or an ultimate reality." Id., at 66a.

The Guidelines prescribe these criteria for determining the amounts of third-party disbursements that will be allowed on behalf of each eligible student organization: the size of the group, its financial self-sufficiency, and the University-wide benefit of its activities. If an organization seeks SAF support, it must submit its bills to the Student Council, which pays the organization's creditors upon determining that the expenses are appropriate. No direct payments are made to the student groups. During the 1990-1991 academic year, 343 student groups qualified as CIO's. One hundred thirty-five of them applied for support from the SAF, and 118 received funding. Fifteen of the groups were funded as "student news, information, opinion, entertainment, or academic communications media groups."

Petitioners' organization, Wide Awake Productions (WAP), qualified as a CIO. Formed by petitioner Ronald Rosenberger and other undergraduates in 1990, WAP was established "to publish a magazine of philosophical and religious expression," "to facilitate discussion which fosters an atmosphere of sensitivity to and tolerance of Christian viewpoints," and "to provide a unifying focus for Christians of multicultural backgrounds." App. 67. WAP publishes Wide Awake: A Christian Perspective at the University of Virginia. The paper's Christian viewpoint was evident from the first issue, in which its editors wrote that the journal "offers a Christian perspective on both personal and community issues, especially those relevant to college students at the University of Virginia." App. 45. The editors committed the paper to a two-fold mission: "to challenge Christians to live, in word and deed, according to the faith they proclaim and to encourage students to consider what a personal relationship with Jesus Christ means." Ibid. The first issue had articles about racism, crisis pregnancy, stress, prayer, C. S. Lewis' ideas about evil and free will, and reviews of religious music. In the next two issues, Wide Awake featured stories about homosexuality, Christian missionary work, and eating disorders, as well as music reviews and interviews with University professors. Each page of Wide Awake, and the end of each article or review, is marked by a cross. The advertisements carried in Wide Awake also reveal the Christian perspective of the journal. For the most part, the advertisers are churches, centers for Christian study, or Christian bookstores. By June 1992, WAP had distributed about 5,000 copies of Wide Awake to University students, free of charge.

WAP had acquired CIO status soon after it was organized. This is an important consideration in this case, for had it been a "religious organization," WAP would not have been accorded CIO status. As defined by the Guidelines, a "religious organization" is "an organization whose purpose is to practice a devotion to an acknowledged ultimate reality or deity." App. to Pet. for Cert. 66a. At no stage in this controversy has the University contended that WAP is such an organization.

A few months after being given CIO status, WAP requested the SAF to pay its printer $ 5,862 for the costs of printing its newspaper. The Appropriations Committee of the Student Council denied WAP's request on the ground that Wide Awake was a "religious activity" within the meaning of the Guidelines, i. e., that the newspaper "promoted or manifested a particular belief in or about a deity or an ultimate reality." Ibid. It made its determination after examining the first issue. App. 54. WAP appealed the denial to the full Student Council, contending that WAP met all the applicable Guidelines and that denial of SAF support on the basis of the magazine's religious perspective violated the Constitution. The appeal was denied without further comment, and WAP appealed to the next level, the Student Activities Committee. In a letter signed by the Dean of Students, the committee sustained the denial of funding. App. 55.

Having no further recourse within the University structure, WAP, Wide Awake, and three of its editors and members filed suit in the United States District Court for the Western District of Virginia, challenging the SAF's action as violative of Rev. Stat. § 1979, 42 U.S.C. § 1983. They alleged that refusal to authorize payment of the printing costs of the publication, solely on the basis of its religious editorial viewpoint, violated their rights to freedom of speech and press, to the free exercise of religion, and to equal protection of the law. They relied also upon Article I of the Virginia Constitution and the Virginia Act for Religious Freedom, Va. Code Ann. § § 57-1, 57-2 (1986 and Supp. 1994), but did not pursue those theories on appeal. The suit sought damages for the costs of printing the paper, injunctive and declaratory relief, and attorney's fees.

On cross-motions for summary judgment, the District Court ruled for the University, holding that denial of SAF support was not an impermissible content or viewpoint discrimination against petitioners' speech, and that the University's Establishment Clause concern over its "religious activities" was a sufficient justification for denying payment to third-party contractors. The court did not issue a definitive ruling on whether reimbursement, had it been made here, would or would not have violated the Establishment Clause. 795 F. Supp. 175, 181-182 (WD Va. 1992).

The United States Court of Appeals for the Fourth Circuit, in disagreement with the District Court, held that the Guidelines did discriminate on the basis of content. It ruled that, while the State need not underwrite speech, there was a presumptive violation of the Speech Clause when viewpoint discrimination was invoked to deny third-party payment otherwise available to CIO's. 18 F.3d 269, 279-281 (1994). The Court of Appeals affirmed the judgment of the District Court nonetheless, concluding that the discrimination by the University was justified by the "compelling interest in maintaining strict separation of church and state." Id., at 281. We granted certiorari. 513 U.S. 959 (1994).

II

It is axiomatic that the government may not regulate speech based on its substantive content or the message it conveys. Police Dept. of Chicago v. Mosley, 408 U.S. 92, 96, 33 L. Ed. 2d 212, 92 S. Ct. 2286 (1972). Other principles follow from this precept. In the realm of private speech or expression, government regulation may not favor one speaker over another. Members of City Council of Los Angeles v. Taxpayers for Vincent, 466 U.S. 789, 804, 80 L. Ed. 2d 772, 104 S. Ct. 2118 (1984). Discrimination against speech because of its message is presumed to be unconstitutional. See Turner Broadcasting System, Inc. v. FCC, 512 U.S. 622, 641-643, 129 L. Ed. 2d 497, 114 S. Ct. 2445 (1994). These rules informed our determination that the government offends the First Amendment when it imposes financial burdens on certain speakers based on the content of their expression. Simon & Schuster, Inc. v. Members of N. Y. State Crime Victims Bd., 502 U.S. 105, 116 L. Ed. 2d 476, 112 S. Ct. 501, 115 (1991). When the government targets not subject matter, but particular views taken by speakers on a subject, the violation of the First Amendment is all the more blatant. See R. A. V. v. St. Paul, 505 U.S. 377, 391, 120 L. Ed. 2d 305, 112 S. Ct. 2538 (1992). Viewpoint discrimination is thus an egregious form of content discrimination. The government must abstain from regulating speech when the specific motivating ideology or the opinion or perspective of the speaker is the rationale for the restriction. See Perry Ed. Assn. v. Perry Local Educators' Assn., 460 U.S. 37, 46, 74 L. Ed. 2d 794, 103 S. Ct. 948 (1983).

These principles provide the framework forbidding the State from exercising viewpoint discrimination, even when the limited public forum is one of its own creation. In a case involving a school district's provision of school facilities for private uses, we declared that "there is no question that the District, like the private owner of property, may legally preserve the property under its control for the use to which it is dedicated." Lamb's Chapel v. Center Moriches Union Free School Dist., 508 U.S. 384, 390, 124 L. Ed. 2d 352, 113 S. Ct. 2141 (1993). The necessities of confining a forum to the limited and legitimate purposes for which it was created may justify the State in reserving it for certain groups or for the discussion of certain topics. See, e. g., Cornelius v. NAACP Legal Defense & Ed. Fund, Inc., 473 U.S. 788, 806, 87 L. Ed. 2d 567, 105 S. Ct. 3439 (1985); Perry Ed. Assn., supra, at 49. Once it has opened a limited forum, however, the State must respect the lawful boundaries it has itself set. The State may not exclude speech where its distinction is not "reasonable in light of the purpose served by the forum," Cornelius, supra, at 804-806; see also Perry Ed. Assn., supra, at 46, 49, nor may it discriminate against speech on the basis of its viewpoint,

Lamb's Chapel, supra, at 392-393; see also Perry Ed. Assn., supra, at 46; R. A. V., supra, at 386-388, 391-393; cf. Texas v. Johnson, 491 U.S. 397, 414-415, 105 L. Ed. 2d 342, 109 S. Ct. 2533 (1989). Thus, in determining whether the State is acting to preserve the limits of the forum it has created so that the exclusion of a class of speech is legitimate, we have observed a distinction between, on the one hand, content discrimination, which may be permissible if it preserves the purposes of that limited forum, and, on the other hand, viewpoint discrimination, which is presumed impermissible when directed against speech otherwise within the forum's limitations. See Perry Ed. Assn., supra, at 46.

The SAF is a forum more in a metaphysical than in a spatial or geographic sense, but the same principles are applicable. See, e.g., Perry Ed. Assn., supra, at 46-47 (forum analysis of a school mail system); Cornelius, supra, at 801 (forum analysis of charitable contribution program). The most recent and most apposite case is our decision in Lamb's Chapel, supra. There, a school district had opened school facilities for use after school hours by community groups for a wide variety of social, civic, and recreational purposes. The district, however, had enacted a formal policy against opening facilities to groups for religious purposes. Invoking its policy, the district rejected a request from a group desiring to show a film series addressing various child-rearing questions from a "Christian perspective." There was no indication in the record in Lamb's Chapel that the request to use the school facilities was "denied, for any reason other than the fact that the presentation would have been from a religious perspective." 508 U.S. at 393-394. Our conclusion was unanimous: "It discriminates on the basis of viewpoint to permit school property to be used for the presentation of all views about family issues and child rearing except those dealing with the subject matter from a religious standpoint." Id., at 393.

The University does acknowledge (as it must in light of our precedents) that "ideologically driven attempts to suppress a particular point of view are presumptively unconstitutional in funding, as in other contexts," but insists that this case does not present that issue because the Guidelines draw lines based on content, not viewpoint. Brief for Respondents 17, n. 10. As we have noted, discrimination against one set of views or ideas is but a subset or particular instance of the more general phenomenon of content discrimination. See, e.g., R. A. V., supra, at 391. And, it must be acknowledged, the distinction is not a precise one. It is, in a sense, something of an understatement to speak of religious thought and discussion as just a viewpoint, as distinct from a comprehensive body of thought. The nature of our origins and destiny and their dependence upon the existence of a divine being have been subjects of philosophic inquiry throughout human history. We conclude, nonetheless, that here, as in Lamb's Chapel, viewpoint discrimination is the proper way to interpret the University's objections to Wide Awake. By the very terms of the SAF prohibition, the University does not exclude religion as a subject matter but selects for disfavored treatment those student journalistic efforts with religious editorial viewpoints. Religion may be a vast area of inquiry, but it also provides, as it did here, a specific premise, a perspective, a standpoint from which a variety of subjects may be discussed and considered. The prohibited perspective, not the general subject matter, resulted in the refusal to make third-party payments, for the subjects discussed were otherwise within the approved category of publications.

The dissent's assertion that no viewpoint discrimination occurs because the Guidelines discriminate against an entire class of viewpoints reflects an insupportable assumption that all debate is bipolar and that antireligious speech is the only response to religious speech. Our understanding of the complex and multifaceted nature of public discourse has not embraced such a contrived description of the marketplace of ideas. If the topic of debate is, for example, racism, then exclusion of several views on that problem is just as offensive to the First Amendment as exclusion of only one. It is as objectionable to exclude both a theistic and an atheistic perspective on the debate as it is to exclude one, the other, or yet another political, economic, or social viewpoint. The dissent's declaration that debate is not skewed so long as multiple voices are silenced is simply wrong; the debate is skewed in multiple ways.

The University's denial of WAP's request for third-party payments in the present case is based upon viewpoint discrimination not unlike the discrimination the school district relied upon in Lamb's Chapel and that we found invalid. The church group in Lamb's Chapel would have been qualified as a social or civic organization, save for its religious purposes. Furthermore, just as the school district in Lamb's Chapel pointed to nothing but the religious views of the group as the rationale for excluding its message, so in this case the University justifies its denial of SAF participation to WAP on the ground that the contents of Wide Awake reveal an avowed religious perspective. See supra, at 827. It bears only passing mention that the dissent's attempt to distinguish Lamb's Chapel is entirely without support in the law. Relying on the transcript of oral argument, the dissent seems to argue that we found viewpoint discrimination in that case because the government excluded Christian, but not atheistic, viewpoints from being expressed in the forum there. Post, at 897-898, and n. 13. The Court relied on no such distinction in holding that discriminating against religious speech was discriminating on the basis of viewpoint. There is no indication in the opinion of the Court (which, unlike an advocate's statements at oral argument, is the law) that exclusion or inclusion of other religious or antireligious voices from that forum had any bearing on its decision.

The University tries to escape the consequences of our holding in Lamb's Chapel by urging that this case involves the provision of funds rather than access to facilities. The University begins with the unremarkable proposition that the State must have substantial discretion in determining how to allocate scarce resources to accomplish its educational mission. Citing our decisions in Rust v. Sullivan, 500 U.S. 173, 114 L. Ed. 2d 233, 111 S. Ct. 1759 (1991), Regan v. Taxation with Representation of Wash., 461 U.S. 540, 76 L. Ed. 2d 129, 103 S. Ct. 1997 (1983), and Widmar v. Vincent, 454 U.S. 263, 70 L. Ed. 2d 440, 102 S. Ct. 269 (1981), the University argues that content-based funding decisions are both inevitable and lawful. Were the reasoning of Lamb's Chapel to apply to funding decisions as well as to those involving access to facilities, it is urged, its holding "would become a judicial juggernaut, constitutionalizing the ubiquitous content-based decisions that schools, colleges, and other government entities routinely make in the allocation of public funds." Brief for Respondents 16.

To this end the University relies on our assurance in Widmar v. Vincent, supra. There, in the course of striking down a public university's exclusion of religious groups from use of school facilities made available to all other student groups, we stated: "Nor do we question the right of the University to make academic judgments as to how best to allocate scarce resources." 454 U.S. at 276. The quoted language in Widmar was but a proper recognition of the principle that when the State is the speaker, it may make content-based choices. When the University determines the content of the education it provides, it is the University speaking, and we have permitted the government to regulate the content of what is or is not expressed when it is the speaker or when it enlists private entities to convey its own message. In the same vein, in Rust v. Sullivan, supra, we upheld the government's prohibition on abortion-related advice applicable to recipients of federal funds for family planning counseling. There, the government did not create a program to encourage private speech but instead used private speakers to transmit specific information pertaining to its own program. We recognized that when the government appropriates public funds to promote a particular policy of its own it is entitled to say what it wishes. 500 U.S. at 194. When the government disburses public funds to private entities to convey a governmental message, it may take legitimate and appropriate steps to ensure that its message is neither garbled nor distorted by the grantee. See id., at 196-200.

It does not follow, however, and we did not suggest in Widmar, that viewpoint-based restrictions are proper when the University does not itself speak or subsidize transmittal of a message it favors but instead expends funds to encourage a diversity of views from private speakers. A holding that the University may not discriminate based on the viewpoint of private persons whose speech it facilitates does not restrict the University's own speech, which is controlled by different principles. See, e.g., Board of Ed. of Westside Community Schools (Dist. 66) v. Mergens, 496 U.S. 226, 250, 110 L. Ed. 2d 191, 110 S. Ct. 2356 (1990); Hazelwood School Dist. v. Kuhlmeier, 484 U.S. 260, 270-272, 98 L. Ed. 2d 592, 108 S. Ct. 562 (1988). For that reason, the University's reliance on Regan v. Taxation with Representation of Wash., supra, is inapposite as well. Regan involved a challenge to Congress' choice to grant tax deductions for contributions made to veterans' groups engaged in lobbying, while denying that favorable status to other charities which pursued lobbying efforts. Although acknowledging that the Government is not required to subsidize the exercise of fundamental rights, see 461 U.S. at 545-546, we reaffirmed the requirement of viewpoint neutrality in the Government's provision of financial benefits by observing that "the case would be different if Congress were to discriminate invidiously in its subsidies in such a way as to 'aim at the suppression of dangerous ideas,'" see id., at 548 (quoting Cammarano v. United States, 358 U.S. 498, 513, 3 L. Ed. 2d 462, 79 S. Ct. 524 (1959), in turn quoting Speiser v. Randall, 357 U.S. 513, 519, 2 L. Ed. 2d 1460, 78 S. Ct. 1332 (1958)). Regan relied on a distinction based on preferential treatment of certain speakers—veterans organizations—and not a distinction based on the content or messages of those groups' speech. 461 U.S. at 548; cf. Perry Ed. Assn., 460 U.S. at 49. The University's regulation now before us, however, has a speech-based restriction as its sole rationale and operative principle.

The distinction between the University's own favored message and the private speech of students is evident in the case before us. The University itself has taken steps to ensure the distinction in the agreement each CIO must sign. See supra, at 824. The University declares that the student groups eligible for SAF support are not the University's agents, are not subject to its control, and are not its responsibility. Having offered to pay the third-party contractors on behalf of private speakers who convey their own messages, the University may not silence the expression of selected viewpoints.

The University urges that, from a constitutional standpoint, funding of speech differs from provision of access to facilities because money is scarce and physical facilities are not. Beyond the fact that in any given case this proposition might not be true as an empirical matter, the underlying premise that the University could discriminate based on viewpoint if demand for space exceeded its availability is wrong as well. The government cannot justify viewpoint discrimination among private speakers on the economic fact of scarcity. Had the meeting rooms in Lamb's Chapel been scarce, had the demand been greater than the supply, our decision would have been no different. It would have been incumbent on the State, of course, to ration or allocate the scarce resources on some acceptable neutral principle; but nothing in our decision indicated that scarcity would give the State the right to exercise viewpoint discrimination that is otherwise impermissible.

Vital First Amendment speech principles are at stake here. The first danger to liberty lies in granting the State the power to examine publications to determine whether or not they are based on some ultimate idea and, if so, for the State to classify them. The second, and corollary, danger is to speech from the chilling of individual thought and expression. That danger is especially real in the University setting, where the State acts against a background and tradition of thought and experiment that is at the center of our intellectual and philosophic tradition. See Healy v. James, 408 U.S. 169, 180-181, 33 L. Ed. 2d 266, 92 S. Ct. 2338 (1972); Keyishian v. Board of Regents of Univ. of State of N. Y., 385 U.S. 589, 603, 17 L. Ed. 2d 629, 87 S. Ct. 675 (1967); Sweezy v. New Hampshire, 354 U.S. 234, 250, 1 L. Ed. 2d 1311, 77 S. Ct. 1203 (1957). In ancient Athens, and, as Europe entered into a new period of intellectual awakening, in places like Bologna, Oxford, and Paris, universities began as voluntary and spontaneous assemblages or concourses for students to speak and to write and to learn. See generally R. Palmer & J. Colton, A History of the Modern World 39 (7th ed. 1992). The quality and creative power of student intellectual life to this day remains a vital measure of a school's influence and attainment. For the University, by regulation, to cast disapproval on particular viewpoints of its students risks the suppression of free speech and creative inquiry in one of the vital centers for the Nation's intellectual life, its college and university campuses.

The Guideline invoked by the University to deny third-party contractor payments on behalf of WAP effects a sweeping restriction on student thought and student inquiry in the context of University sponsored publications. The prohibition on funding on behalf of publications that "primarily promote or manifest a particular belief in or about a deity or an ultimate reality," in its ordinary and common-sense meaning, has a vast potential reach. The term "promotes" as used here would comprehend any writing advocating a philosophic position that rests upon a belief in a deity or ultimate reality. See Webster's Third New International Dictionary 1815 (1961) (defining "promote" as "to contribute to the growth, enlargement, or prosperity of: further, encourage"). And the term "manifests" would bring within the scope of the prohibition any writing that is explicable as resting upon a premise that presupposes the existence of a deity or ultimate reality. See id., at 1375 (defining "manifest" as "to show plainly: make palpably evident or certain by showing or displaying"). Were the prohibition applied with much vigor at all, it would bar funding of essays by hypothetical student contributors named Plato, Spinoza, and Descartes. And if the regulation covers, as the University says it does, see Tr. of Oral Arg. 18-19, those student journalistic efforts that primarily manifest or promote a belief that there is no deity and no ultimate reality, then undergraduates named Karl Marx, Bertrand Russell, and Jean-Paul Sartre would likewise have some of their major essays excluded from student publications. If any manifestation of beliefs in first principles disqualifies the writing, as seems to be the case, it is indeed difficult to name renowned thinkers whose writings would be accepted, save perhaps for articles disclaiming all connection to their ultimate philosophy. Plato could contrive perhaps to submit an acceptable essay on making pasta or peanut butter cookies, provided he did not point out their (necessary) imperfections.

Based on the principles we have discussed, we hold that the regulation invoked to deny SAF support, both in its terms and in its application to these petitioners, is a denial of their right of free speech guaranteed by the First Amendment. It remains to be considered whether the violation following from the University's action is excused by the necessity of complying with the Constitution's prohibition against state establishment of religion. We turn to that question.

III

Before its brief on the merits in this Court, the University had argued at all stages of the litigation that inclusion of WAP's contractors in SAF funding authorization would violate the Establishment Clause. Indeed, that is the ground on which the University prevailed in the Court of Appeals. We granted certiorari on this question: "Whether the Establishment Clause compels a state university to exclude an otherwise eligible student publication from participation in the student activities fund, solely on the basis of its religious viewpoint, where such exclusion would violate the Speech and Press Clauses if the viewpoint of the publication were nonreligious." Pet. for Cert. i. The University now seems to have abandoned this position, contending that "the fundamental objection to petitioners' argument is not that it implicates the Establishment Clause but that it would defeat the ability of public education at all levels to control the use of public funds." Brief for Respondents 29; see id., at 27-29, and n. 17; Tr. of Oral Arg. 14. That the University itself no longer presses the Establishment Clause claim is some indication that it lacks force; but as the Court of Appeals rested its judgment on the point and our dissenting colleagues would find it determinative, it must be addressed.

The Court of Appeals ruled that withholding SAF support from Wide Awake contravened the Speech Clause of the First Amendment, but proceeded to hold that the University's action was justified by the necessity of avoiding a violation of the Establishment Clause, an interest it found compelling. 18 F.3d at 281. Recognizing that this Court has regularly "sanctioned awards of direct nonmonetary benefits to religious groups where government has created open fora to which all similarly situated organizations are invited," id., at 286 (citing Widmar, 454 U.S. at 277), the Fourth Circuit asserted that direct monetary subsidization of religious organizations and projects is "a beast of an entirely different color," 18 F.3d at 286. The court declared that the Establishment Clause would not permit the use of public funds to support "a specifically religious activity in an otherwise substantially secular setting." Id., at 285 (quoting Hunt v. McNair, 413 U.S. 734, 743, 37 L. Ed. 2d 923, 93 S. Ct. 2868 (1973) (emphasis deleted)). It reasoned that because Wide Awake is "a journal pervasively devoted to the discussion and advancement of an avowedly Christian theological and personal philosophy," the University's provision of SAF funds for its publication would "send an unmistakably clear signal that the

University of Virginia supports Christian values and wishes to promote the wide promulgation of such values." 18 F.3d at 286.

If there is to be assurance that the Establishment Clause retains its force in guarding against those governmental actions it was intended to prohibit, we must in each case inquire first into the purpose and object of the governmental action in question and then into the practical details of the program's operation. Before turning to these matters, however, we can set forth certain general principles that must bear upon our determination.

A central lesson of our decisions is that a significant factor in upholding governmental programs in the face of Establishment Clause attack is their neutrality towards religion. We have decided a series of cases addressing the receipt of government benefits where religion or religious views are implicated in some degree. The first case in our modern Establishment Clause jurisprudence was Everson v. Board of Ed. of Ewing, 330 U.S. 1, 91 L. Ed. 711, 67 S. Ct. 504 (1947). There we cautioned that in enforcing the prohibition against laws respecting establishment of religion, we must "be sure that we do not inadvertently prohibit [the government] from extending its general state law benefits to all its citizens without regard to their religious belief." Id., at 16. We have held that the guarantee of neutrality is respected, not offended, when the government, following neutral criteria and evenhanded policies, extends benefits to recipients whose ideologies and viewpoints, including religious ones, are broad and diverse. See Board of Ed. of Kiryas Joel Village School Dist. v. Grumet, 512 U.S. 687, 704, 129 L. Ed. 2d 546, 114 S. Ct. 2481 (1994) (SOUTER, J.) ("The principle is well grounded in our case law [and] we have frequently relied explicitly on the general availability of any benefit provided religious groups or individuals in turning aside Establishment Clause challenges"); Witters v. Washington Dept. of Servs. for Blind, 474 U.S. 481, 487-488, 88 L. Ed. 2d 846, 106 S. Ct. 748 (1986); Mueller v. Allen, 463 U.S. 388, 398-399, 77 L. Ed. 2d 721, 103 S. Ct. 3062 (1983); Widmar, supra, at 274-275. More than once have we rejected the position that the Establishment Clause even justifies, much less requires, a refusal to extend free speech rights to religious speakers who participate in broad-reaching government programs neutral in design. See Lamb's Chapel, 508 U.S. at 393-394; Mergens, 496 U.S. at 248, 252; Widmar, supra, at 274-275.

The governmental program here is neutral toward religion. There is no suggestion that the University created it to advance religion or adopted some ingenious device with the purpose of aiding a religious cause. The object of the SAF is to open a forum for speech and to support various student enterprises, including the publication of newspapers, in recognition of the diversity and creativity of student life. The University's SAF Guidelines have a separate classification for, and do not make third-party payments on behalf of, "religious organizations," which are those "whose purpose is to practice a devotion to an acknowledged ultimate reality or deity." Pet. for Cert. 66a. The category of support here is for "student news, information, opinion, entertainment, or academic communications media groups," of which Wide Awake was 1 of 15 in the 1990 school year. WAP did not seek a subsidy because of its Christian editorial viewpoint; it sought funding as a student journal, which it was.

The neutrality of the program distinguishes the student fees from a tax levied for the direct support of a church or group of churches. A tax of that sort, of course, would run contrary to Establishment Clause concerns dating from the earliest days of the Republic. The apprehensions of our predecessors involved the levying of taxes upon the public for the sole and exclusive purpose of establishing and supporting specific sects. The exaction here, by contrast, is a student activity fee designed to reflect the reality that student life in its many dimensions includes the necessity of wide-ranging speech and inquiry and that student expression is an integral part of the University's educational mission. The fee is mandatory, and we do not have before us the question whether an objecting student has the First Amendment right to demand a pro rata return to the extent the fee is expended for speech to which he or she does not subscribe. See Keller v. State Bar of Cal., 496 U.S. 1, 15-16, 110 L. Ed.

2d 1, 110 S. Ct. 2228 (1990); Abood v. Detroit Bd. of Ed., 431 U.S. 209, 235-236, 52 L. Ed. 2d 261, 97 S. Ct. 1782 (1977). We must treat it, then, as an exaction upon the students. But the $14 paid each semester by the students is not a general tax designed to raise revenue for the University. See United States v. Butler, 297 U.S. 1, 61, 80 L. Ed. 477, 56 S. Ct. 312 (1936) ("A tax, in the general understanding of the term, and as used in the Constitution, signifies an exaction for the support of the Government"); see also Head Money Cases, 112 U.S. 580, 595-596, 28 L. Ed. 798, 5 S. Ct. 247 (1884). The SAF cannot be used for unlimited purposes, much less the illegitimate purpose of supporting one religion. Much like the arrangement in Widmar, the money goes to a special fund from which any group of students with CIO status can draw for purposes consistent with the University's educational mission; and to the extent the student is interested in speech, withdrawal is permitted to cover the whole spectrum of speech, whether it manifests a religious view, an antireligious view, or neither. Our decision, then, cannot be read as addressing an expenditure from a general tax fund. Here, the disbursements from the fund go to private contractors for the cost of printing that which is protected under the Speech Clause of the First Amendment. This is a far cry from a general public assessment designed and effected to provide financial support for a church.

Government neutrality is apparent in the State's overall scheme in a further meaningful respect. The program respects the critical difference "between government speech endorsing religion, which the Establishment Clause forbids, and private speech endorsing religion, which the Free Speech and Free Exercise Clauses protect." Mergens, supra, at 250 (opinion of O'CONNOR, J.). In this case, "the government has not fostered or encouraged" any mistaken impression that the student newspapers speak for the University. Capitol Square Review and Advisory Bd. v. Pinette, ante, at 766. The University has taken pains to disassociate itself from the private speech involved in this case. The Court of Appeals' apparent concern that Wide Awake's religious orientation would be attributed to the University is not a plausible fear, and there is no real likelihood that the [*842] speech in question is being either endorsed or coerced by the State, see Lee v. Weisman, 505 U.S. 577, 587, 120 L. Ed. 2d 467, 112 S. Ct. 2649 (1992); Witters, supra, at 489 (citing Lynch v. Donnelly, 465 U.S. 668, 688, 79 L. Ed. 2d 604, 104 S. Ct. 1355 (1984) (O'CONNOR, J., concurring)); see also Witters, supra, at 493 (O'CONNOR, J., concurring in part and concurring in judgment) (citing Lynch, supra, at 690 (O'CONNOR, J., concurring)).

The Court of Appeals (and the dissent) are correct to extract from our decisions the principle that we have recognized special Establishment Clause dangers where the government makes direct money payments to sectarian institutions, citing Roemer v. Board of Public Works of Md., 426 U.S. 736, 747, 49 L. Ed. 2d 179, 96 S. Ct. 2337 (1976); Bowen v. Kendrick, 487 U.S. 589, 614-615, 101 L. Ed. 2d 520, 108 S. Ct. 2562 (1988); Hunt v. McNair, 413 U.S. at 742; Tilton v. Richardson, 403 U.S. 672, 679-680, 29 L. Ed. 2d 790, 91 S. Ct. 2091 (1971); Board of Ed. of Central School Dist. No. 1 v. Allen, 392 U.S. 236, 20 L. Ed. 2d 1060, 88 S. Ct. 1923 (1968). The error is not in identifying the principle, but in believing that it controls this case. Even assuming that WAP is no different from a church and that its speech is the same as the religious exercises conducted in Widmar (two points much in doubt), the Court of Appeals decided a case that was, in essence, not before it, and the dissent would have us do the same. We do not confront a case where, even under a neutral program that includes nonsectarian recipients, the government is making direct money payments to an institution or group that is engaged in religious activity. Neither the Court of Appeals nor the dissent, we believe, takes sufficient cognizance of the undisputed fact that no public funds flow directly to WAP's coffers.

It does not violate the Establishment Clause for a public university to grant access to its facilities on a religion-neutral basis to a wide spectrum of student groups, including groups that use meeting rooms for sectarian activities, accompanied by some devotional exercises. See Widmar, 454 U.S. at 269; Mergens, 496 U.S. at 252.

This is so even where the upkeep, maintenance, and repair of the facilities attributed to those uses is paid from a student activities fund to which students are required to contribute. Widmar, supra, at 265. The government usually acts by spending money. Even the provision of a meeting room, as in Mergens and Widmar, involved governmental expenditure, if only in the form of electricity and heating or cooling costs. The error made by the Court of Appeals, as well as by the dissent, lies in focusing on the money that is undoubtedly expended by the government, rather than on the nature of the benefit received by the recipient. If the expenditure of governmental funds is prohibited whenever those funds pay for a service that is, pursuant to a religion-neutral program, used by a group for sectarian purposes, then Widmar, Mergens, and Lamb's Chapel would have to be overruled. Given our holdings in these cases, it follows that a public university may maintain its own computer facility and give student groups access to that facility, including the use of the printers, on a religion neutral, say first-come-first-served, basis. If a religious student organization obtained access on that religion-neutral basis and used a computer to compose or a printer or copy machine to print speech with a religious content or viewpoint, the State's action in providing the group with access would no more violate the Establishment Clause than would giving those groups access to an assembly hall. See Lamb's Chapel v. Center Moriches

Union Free School Dist., 508 U.S. 384, 124 L. Ed. 2d 352, 113 S. Ct. 2141 (1993); Widmar, supra; Mergens, supra. There is no difference in logic or principle, and no difference of constitutional significance, between a school using its funds to operate a facility to which students have access, and a school paying a third-party contractor to operate the facility on its behalf. The latter occurs here. The University provides printing services to a broad spectrum of student newspapers qualified as CIO's by reason of their officers and membership. Any benefit to religion is incidental to the government's provision of secular services for secular purposes on a religion-neutral basis. Printing is a routine, secular, and recurring attribute of student life.

By paying outside printers, the University in fact attains a further degree of separation from the student publication, for it avoids the duties of supervision, escapes the costs of upkeep, repair, and replacement attributable to student use, and has a clear record of costs. As a result, and as in Widmar, the University can charge the SAF, and not the taxpayers as a whole, for the discrete activity in question. It would be formalistic for us to say that the University must forfeit these advantages and provide the services itself in order to comply with the Establishment Clause. It is, of course, true that if the State pays a church's bills it is subsidizing it, and we must guard against this abuse. That is not a danger here, based on the considerations we have advanced and for the additional reason that the student publication is not a religious institution, at least in the usual sense of that term as used in our case law, and it is not a religious organization as used in the University's own regulations. It is instead a publication involved in a pure forum for the expression of ideas, ideas that would be both incomplete and chilled were the Constitution to be interpreted to require that state officials and courts scan the publication to ferret out views that principally manifest a belief in a divine being.

Were the dissent's view to become law, it would require the University, in order to avoid a constitutional violation, to scrutinize the content of student speech, lest the expression in question—speech otherwise protected by the Constitution—contain too great a religious content. The dissent, in fact, anticipates such censorship as "crucial" in distinguishing between "works characterized by the evangelism of Wide Awake and writing that merely happens to express views that a given religion might approve." Post, at 896. That eventuality raises the specter of governmental censorship, to ensure that all student writings and publications meet some baseline standard of secular orthodoxy. To impose that standard on student speech at a university is to imperil the very sources of free speech and expression. As we recognized in Widmar, official censorship would be far more inconsistent with the Establishment Clause's dictates than would governmental provision of secular printing services on a religion-blind basis.

"The dissent fails to establish that the distinction [between 'religious' speech and speech 'about' religion] has intelligible content. There is no indication when 'singing hymns, reading scripture, and teaching biblical principles' cease to be 'singing, teaching, and reading'-- all apparently forms of 'speech,' despite their religious subject matter--and become unprotected 'worship.' . . .

"Even if the distinction drew an arguably principled line, it is highly doubtful that it would lie within the judicial competence to administer. Merely to draw the distinction would require the university--and ultimately the courts--to inquire into the significance of words and practices to different religious faiths, and in varying circumstances by the same faith. Such inquiries would tend inevitably to entangle the State with religion in a manner forbidden by our cases. E. g., Walz v. Tax Comm'n of City of New York, 397 U.S. 664, 25 L. Ed. 2d 697, 90 S. Ct. 1409 (1970)." 454 U.S. at 269-270, n. 6 (citations omitted).

* * *

To obey the Establishment Clause, it was not necessary for the University to deny eligibility to student publications because of their viewpoint. The neutrality commanded of the State by the separate Clauses of the

First Amendment was compromised by the University's course of action. The viewpoint discrimination inherent in the University's regulation required public officials to scan and interpret student publications to discern their underlying philosophic assumptions respecting religious theory and belief. That course of action was a denial of the right of free speech and would risk fostering a pervasive bias or hostility to religion, which could undermine the very neutrality the Establishment Clause requires. There is no Establishment Clause violation in the University's honoring its duties under the Free Speech Clause.

The judgment of the Court of Appeals must be, and is, reversed.

It is so ordered.

CASE APPENDIX

The following cases were each discussed in the text of the guide. Their precise legal citations (for the scholars among you, or for your attorneys) are below:

U.S. SUPREME COURT CASES

Board of Regents of the University of Wisconsin System v. Southworth, 529 U.S. 217 (2000).

Rosenberger v. Rectors of the University of Virginia, 515 U.S. 819 (1995).

IMPORTANT LOWER COURT DECISIONS

Carroll v. Blinken, 957 F.2d 991 (2d Cir. 1992).

Galda v. Rutgers, 772 F.2d 1060 (3rd Cir.1985).

Gay and Lesbian Students Association v. Gohn, 850 F.2d 361 (8th Cir. 1988).

Smith v. Regents of the University of California, 4 Cal. 4th 843; 844 P.2d 500 (Cal. 1993).

Southworth v. Board of Regents of the University of Wisconsin System, 307 F.3d 566 (7th Cir. 2002).

FIRE's *GUIDES* TO
STUDENT RIGHTS ON CAMPUS
BOARD OF EDITORS

Vivian Berger – Vivian Berger is the Nash Professor of Law Emerita at Columbia Law School. Berger is former New York County Assistant District Attorney and former Assistant Counsel to the NAACP Legal Defense and Educational Fund. She has done significant work in the fields of criminal law and procedure (in particular, the death penalty and habeas corpus) and mediation, and continues to use her expertise in various settings, both public and private. Professor Berger is General Counsel for and National Board Member of the American Civil Liberties Union and has written numerous essays and journal articles on human rights and due process.

T. Kenneth Cribb, Jr. – T. Kenneth Cribb, Jr. is the President of the Intercollegiate Studies Institute, a nonpartisan, educational organization dedicated to furthering the American ideal of ordered liberty on college and university campuses. He served as Counselor to the Attorney General of the United States and later as Assistant to the President for Domestic Affairs during the Reagan administration. Cribb is also President of the Collegiate Network of independent college newspapers. He is former Vice Chairman of the Fulbright Foreign Scholarship Board.

Alan Dershowitz – Alan Dershowitz is the Felix Frankfurter Professor of Law at the Harvard Law School. He is an expert on civil liberties and criminal law and has been described by *Newsweek* as "the nation's most peripatetic civil liberties lawyer and one of its most distinguished defenders of individual rights." Dershowitz is a frequent public commentator on matters of freedom of expression and of due process, and is the author of eighteen books, including, most recently, *Why Terrorism Works: Understanding the Threat, Responding to the Challenge*, and hundreds of magazine and journal articles.

Paul McMasters – Paul McMasters is the First Amendment Ombudsman at the Freedom Forum in Arlington, Virginia. He speaks and writes frequently on all aspects of First Amendment rights, has appeared on various television programs, and has testified before numerous government commissions and congressional committees. Prior to joining the Freedom Forum, McMasters was the Associate Editorial Director of *USA Today*. He is also past National President of the Society of Professional Journalists.

Edwin Meese III – Edwin Meese III holds the Ronald Reagan Chair in Public Policy at the Heritage Foundation. He is also Chairman of Heritage's Center for Legal and Judicial Studies. Meese is a Distinguished Visiting Fellow at the Hoover Institution at Stanford University, and a Distinguished Senior Fellow at The University of London's Institute of United States Studies. He is also Chairman of the governing board at George Mason University in Virginia. Meese served as the 75th Attorney General of the United States under the Reagan administration.

Roger Pilon – Roger Pilon is Vice President for Legal Affairs at the Cato Institute, where he holds the B. Kenneth Simon Chair in Constitutional Studies, directs Cato's Center for Constitutional Studies, and publishes the *Cato Supreme Court Review*. Prior to joining Cato, he held five senior posts in the Reagan administration. He has taught philosophy and law, and was a National Fellow at Stanford's Hoover Institution. Pilon has published widely in moral, political, and legal theory.

Jamin Raskin – Jamin Raskin is Professor of Law at American University Washington College of Law, specializing in constitutional law and the First Amendment. He served as a member of the Clinton-Gore Justice Department Transition Team, as Assistant Attorney General in the Commonwealth of Massachusetts and as General Counsel for the National Rainbow Coalition. Raskin has also been a Teaching Fellow in the Government Department at Harvard University and has won several awards for his scholarly essays and journal articles. He is author of *We the Students* and founder of the Marshall-Brennan Fellows Program, which sends law students into public high schools to teach the Constitution.

Nadine Strossen – Nadine Strossen is President of the American Civil Liberties Union and Professor of Law at New York Law School. Strossen has published approximately 250 works in scholarly and general interest publications, and she is the author of two significant books on the importance of civil liberties to the struggle for equality. She has lectured and practiced extensively in the areas of constitutional law and civil liberties, and is a frequent commentator in the national media on various legal issues.

ABOUT FIRE

FIRE's mission is to defend, sustain, and restore individual rights at America's colleges and universities. These rights include freedom of speech, legal equality, due process, religious liberty, and sanctity of conscience—the essential qualities of civil liberty and human dignity. FIRE's core goals are to protect the unprotected against repressive behavior and partisan policies of all kinds, to educate the public about the threat to individual rights that exists on our campuses, and to lead the way in the necessary and moral effort to preserve the rights of students and faculty to speak their minds, to honor their consciences, and to be treated honestly, fairly, and equally by their institutions.

FIRE is a charitable and educational tax-exempt foundation within the meaning of Section 501 (c) (3) of the Internal Revenue Code. Contributions to FIRE are deductible to the fullest extent provided by tax laws. FIRE is funded entirely through individual donations; we receive no government funding. Please visit **www.thefire.org** for more information about FIRE.